Revolutionary Piano Method

Based on Principles of Instructional Design

Lesson Book Level 1

Leslie M. Young, MFA

© 2019 by Leslie M. Young

www.piano4me.org

Technical Graphics and Digital Layout created by Rykah L. Young

All rights reserved. No part of the material protected by this copyright notice may be reproduced or used in any form or by any means, electronic or mechanical, including photocopying, recording, or by any information storage and retrieval system, without prior written permission of the copyright owner.

Table of Contents

Overview, Instructional Note to the Teacher	2 - 3
Teaching Tips!	4
The Keyboard, The Staff	5 – 8
The Treble Clef, Treble Clef Spaces	9 - 10
Exercises Introducing Treble Spaces F,A,C,E	11 – 12
Play By Touch, Not By Looking	13
Robot Sam	14
Pet Dinosaur	15
Treble Clef Lines	16
Exercises Introducing Treble Lines E, G	17
Good Start!	18
Exercises Introducing Treble Line B	19
High Flying	20
Hey! Diddle, Diddle	22
Exercises Introducing Treble Line D	23
Soda Pop	24
Music Math!	26
Exercises Introducing Treble Line F	27
Campfire Dance	28
Muddy Socks	30
A Dinosaur!	32
The Bass Clef, Bass Clef Spaces	33 – 37
Play By Touch, Not By Looking	38
Twinkle, Twinkle, Little Star	39
Squishy Sneakers	40
Bass Clef Lines	41
Exercises Introducing Bass Lines G,B	42
Bubble Travel	43
Exercises Introducing Bass Line D	44
Don't Be Silly	45
Yankee Doodle	47
Exercises Introducing Bass Line F	48
Fishing with Grandpa	49
This Old Man	51
Exercises Introducing Bass Line A	52
Seaside	53
Pop! Goes the Weasel!	55
Melody and Accompaniment, Grand Staff	57
Soda Pop	58
Mary Had a Little Lamb	59
London Bridge	60
Yankee Doodle	61
Hey! Diddle, Diddle	62
This Old Man	63
Twinkle, Twinkle, Little Star	64

Overview

The Revolutionary Piano Method is like no other published course for learning to play the piano, as it is based on the principles of Instructional Design. Each **Lesson Book** introduces one concept at a time and allows the student to become somewhat proficient before introducing another new concept. The student first learns all treble spaces, then treble lines, followed by bass spaces, then lines. After successfully playing each clef separately, the grand staff is introduced for both hands playing together. Proper notes, rests, and timing appear in Level Two. By methodically increasing one skill at a time, the student should never feel overwhelmed.

The student internalizes a thinking process which enables him to identify lines and spaces and locate their corresponding keys. This cognitive procedure facilitates keyboard playing *without dependence upon hand positioning or fingering derived from five-finger positions.* This is critical to the development of sight-reading skill and is similar to learning to read a language phonetically, rather than memorizing words by sight.

A unique feature is the **Warm-Up!** exercise included with each lesson, which develops the student's skill of playing by touch, rather than constant looking at the piano keyboard for orientation.

The **Theory Book** directly correlates with the **Lesson Book** and reinforces learned concepts through writing experiences, puzzles, and games designed to be interesting and fun so as to increase student enthusiasm and motivation.

The **Fun Book!** provides additional practice material and correlates with the **Lesson Book**. All or most of the songs should be familiar to the student, increasing motivation and interest. For maximum benefit, all books of the same level should be used in correlation. Lesson assignments are stated at the top of each page.

Instructional Note to the Teacher

"Center F", the lowest space on the treble staff, is introduced first in order for the student to establish a point of reference between the staff and the keyboard. Upon that basis the other 3 spaces and their corresponding keys are introduced using the memory aid "FACE" for the 4 treble spaces. Exercises using only these spaces help the student remember these spaces and keys *by saying aloud each letter name* as its key is played. The memory aid "**FACE**" should be referred to as often as needed to prompt the student's thinking process. As treble lines are introduced, *the spaces are used as reference points* in reading line notes and locating line keys on the piano.

For example: To identify the treble "D" line,
write in the spaces "F A C" and
then ask the student, "What letter follows C?"

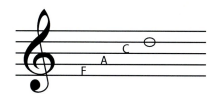

Refrain from writing in letters to the notes themselves, as this will not encourage the thinking process to sight reading. Once the line has been identified, use the space keys on the piano to locate the line key.

For example: To read and play treble line "D",
locate keys "F A C" and
then the line key "D".

For the bass clef, use the memory aid "**All Cows Eat Grass**" for the 4 spaces. To identify the "F" line, write in the spaces "A C E" - then ask the student, "All Cows Eat - Eat for E. . . What letter follows E?"

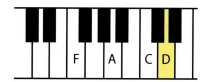

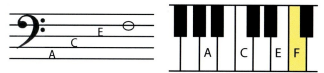

The student should be able to identify spaces and lines and their keys as soon as he has internalized this cognitive process - and then require little or no teacher prompting. Later you may desire to reinforce this method by putting a dot on each space of the staff until reaching the space just under the line to be identified, causing the student to think of the spaces to identify the line.

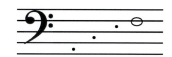

Teaching Tips

ASSIGNMENT PACING: The proficiency level of each student should be considered when assigning practice pages for the week's lesson. Many students are assigned the **Lesson Book** page and its corresponding **Fun Book** song (written at the top of each **Fun Book** page) as their week's assignment. However, if desired, these book assignments could be alternated: the **Lesson Book** page assigned one week – and the **Fun Book** correlating assignment page the next week. **Lesson Book** pages should be assigned <u>before</u> the **Fun Book** songs because new material is introduced in the **Lesson Book** and reinforced in the **Fun Book.**

BLACK KEY GROUP: To reinforce the practice of using the black key groups to locate white keys on the keyboard, the teacher may desire to instruct the student to strike any group of three black keys with either hand and then slide the hand forward to play the white F key to the left of the group. This could be repeated with several groups of three black keys before the lesson as a warm-up exercise.

The student could then strike a group of two black keys with either hand and then slide the hand forward to play the white C key to the left of the group. This could be repeated with several groups of two black keys.

This procedure assists the student in utilizing any black key group in the location of specific white keys. After becoming very familiar with the location of the F and C white keys, these function as starting points for locating other white keys.

BASS STAFF LINE A: The top line of the bass staff could be referred to as "always A…A for always."

Refer to the staff spaces <u>as often as necessary</u> to prompt student indentification of the line notes.
Use the space keys to find the line keys.

The Piano Keyboard   5

The piano is a percussion instrument, which means the player must strike the keys to produce sounds.

The drum and triangle are also percussion instruments.

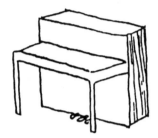 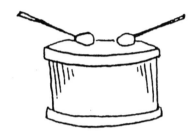 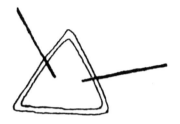

There are 88 keys on the piano keyboard: 36 black keys and 52 white keys. Each key has a letter name, but there are only 7 different letters used to name all the keys:

A B C D E F G

The Keyboard

We will learn the names of the black keys later but use them now to locate the white keys.

Notice that the black keys are in groups of twos and threes.

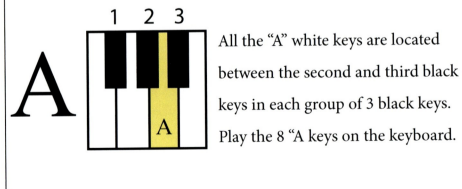

All the "A" white keys are located between the second and third black keys in each group of 3 black keys. Play the 8 "A keys on the keyboard.

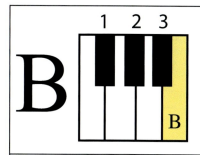

B — All the "B" white keys are located to the right of the third black key in each group of 3 black keys.
Play the 8 "B" keys on the keyboard.

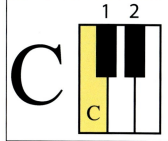

C — All the "C" white keys are located to the left of the first black key in each group of 2 black keys.
Play the 8 "C" keys on the keyboard.

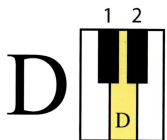

D — All the "D" white keys are located between the 2 black keys in each group of 2 black keys.
Play the 7 "D" keys on the keyboard.

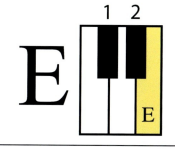

E — All the "E" white keys are located to the right of the second black key in each group of 2 black keys.
Play the 7 "E" keys on the keyboard.

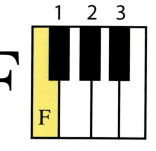

F — All the "F" white keys are located to the left of the first black key in each group of 3 black keys.
Play the 7 "F" keys on the keyboard.

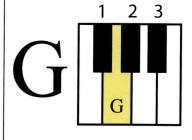

G — All the "G" white keys are located between the first and second black keys in each group of 3 black keys.
Play the 7 "G" keys on the keyboard.

The Staff

8

Piano keys are represented by lines and spaces drawn on paper. Five lines and four spaces grouped together are called a **staff**.

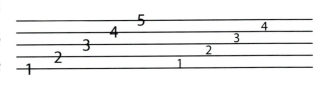

Each line and space is given the letter name of the key it represents on the keyboard.

Look at the letter names of the 5 lines and 4 spaces of the staff:

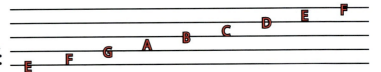

Remember, these 5 lines and 4 spaces represent 9 specific white keys on the keyboard.

The circled "F" space represents the white key "F" which is in the center of the keyboard. We'll call this "center F".

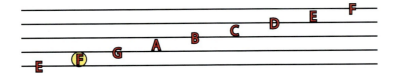

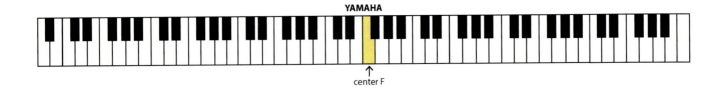

Play this "center F" key on the keyboard. It's in front of the group of 3 black keys which are closest to the center of the keyboard, under the brand name of your piano.

Use Center F to locate the other 8 white keys represented by the staff. **9**
To the left of center F is the lowest line key E.

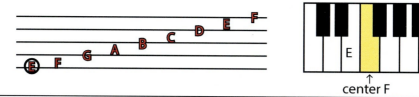

Beginning with this E, play the 9 keys
E F G A B C D E F, saying each letter
name as you play its key.

Use your right hand finger 2 as shown.

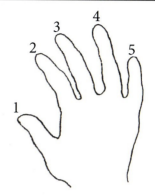

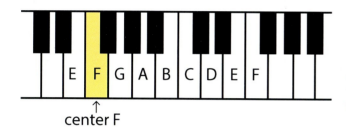

Notice as you play UP the staff, you play UP the keyboard to the right.

The Treble Clef

The **treble clef sign** 𝄞 drawn on the staff means to use the right hand to play the keys. This right hand staff is called the **treble clef**.

Play these 9 keys using your right hand fingers 123 123 123.
Say each letter name as you play its key.

Notice as you play UP the keyboard (left to right), you are reading UP the staff.

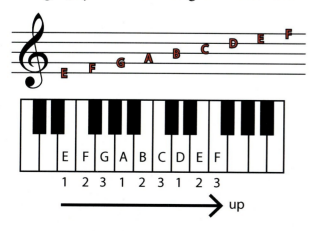

Now play these 9 keys backwards using your right hand fingers 321 321 321.
Say each letter name as you play its key.

As you play DOWN the keyboard (right to left), you are reading DOWN the staff.

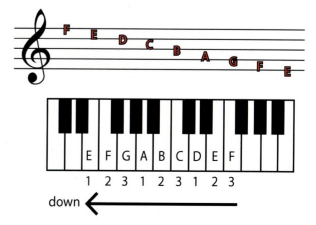

10 The 4 Treble Clef Spaces

To help you locate these keys easily when playing in random order, **let the 4 spaces of the staff be your guide!** The 4 spaces are F A C and E, in order from lowest to highest space. They will be easy to remember because they spell **FACE!**

Play the center F key on the keyboard. **It is the lowest space F on the right hand's treble clef staff.**

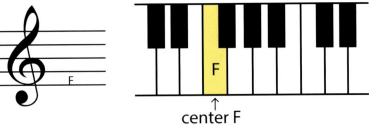

center F

Remember, each line and space of the staff represents a key on the piano keyboard. When you play the keys represented by the 4 spaces of the staff, you will be **skipping over the keys** represented by the 5 lines of the staff.

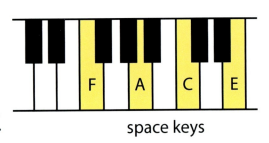

space keys

Play the 4 keys represented by the 4 spaces of the staff, FACE. Use right hand fingers 1235.

"F-A-C-E spells face!"

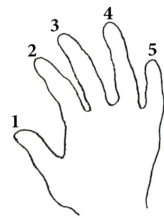

- First play UP, left to right, and say each letter name as you play its key.

- Then play DOWN, right to left, and say each letter name as you play its key.

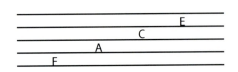

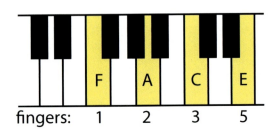

fingers: 1   2   3   5

Play the following exercises. Circles will show you which space keys to play:

Use this fingering!

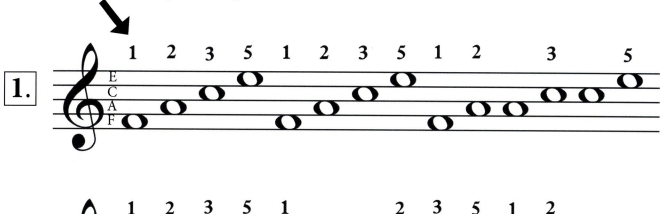

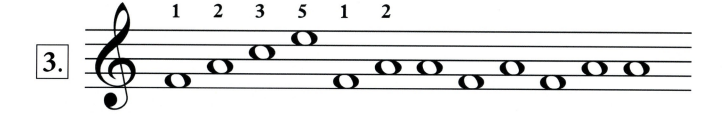

Use this fingering!

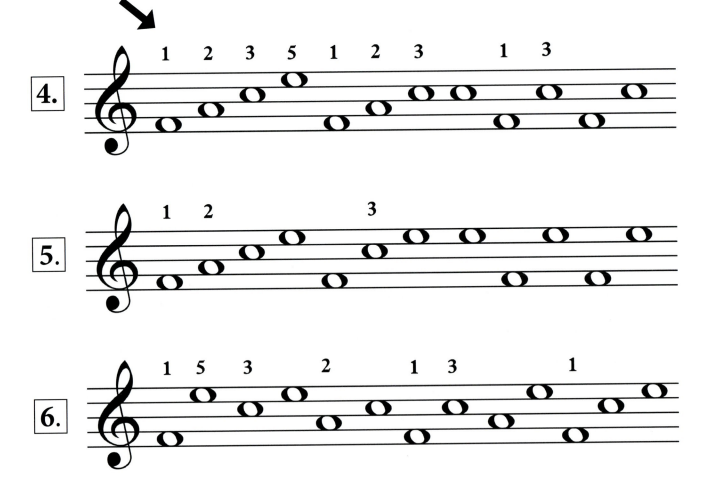

Play By Touch, Not By Looking

13

To help you play more easily and correctly, try these ways to locate the space keys. Try not to look at the keys as much as possible. Then try to play with your eyes closed!

Center F

1. Locate the group of 3 black keys to the right of the center F.

2. Finger 1 bumps the left side of the first black key.

3. Finger 1 slides down toward you and plays the center F key.

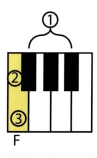

A

1. Locate the group of 3 black keys to the right of the center F.

2. Finger 1 bumps the left side of the first black key and slides toward you on center F.

3. Finger 2 hops over and plays the A key.

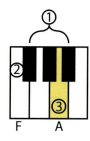

C

1. Locate the group of 2 black keys to the right of the center F.

2. Finger 3 bumps the left side of the first black key.

3. Finger 3 slides toward you and plays the C key.

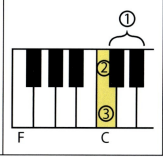

E

1. Locate the group of 2 black keys to the right of the center F.

2. Finger 5 bumps the right side of the second black key.

3. Finger 5 slides toward you and plays the E key.

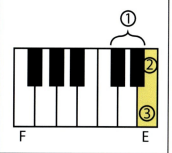

14 Treble Warm-Ups!

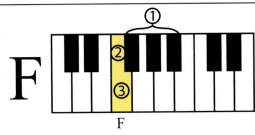

1. Locate center F's group of 3 black keys.
2. Finger 1 bumps the left side of the first black key.
3. Finger 1 slides toward you and plays center F.

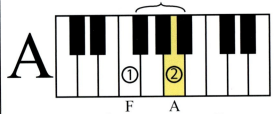

1. Finger 1 locates center F, to the left of the group of 3 black keys.
2. Finger 2 hops over to play the A key.

1. Say each letter name as you play its key.
2. Sing the lyrics as you play.

Robot Sam

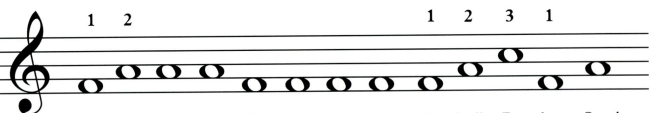

Yes-ter-day down in my base-ment I built Ro-bot Sam!

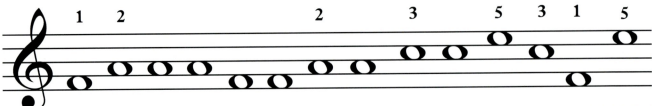

I said, "Hey you real-ly look smart!" He said, "Yes I am! BEEP!"

Treble Warm-Ups!

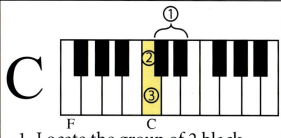

1. Locate the group of 2 black keys to the right of center F.
2. Finger 3 bumps the left side of the first black key.
3. Finger 3 slides toward you and plays the C key.

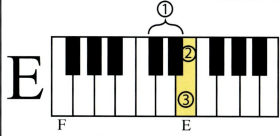

1. Locate the group of 2 black keys to the right of center F.
2. Finger 5 bumps the right side of the second black key.
3. Finger 5 slides toward you and plays the E key.

1. Say each letter name as you play its key.
2. Sing the lyrics as you play.

Pet Dinosaur

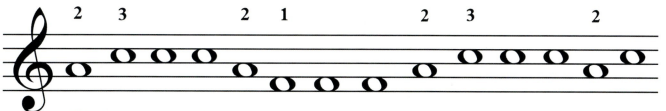

To have a big pet di – no – saur would real – ly be a treat!

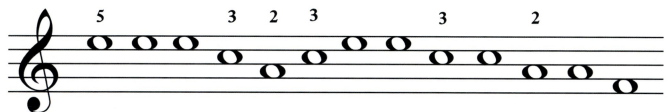

He'd be nice but I had bet – ter watch out for his feet!

16   The Treble Clef Lines

Now that you have learned the space keys F A C E, use them to learn the line keys.

Each line of the treble staff is given the letter name of the key it represents on the keyboard.
Look at the letter names of the 5 lines of the staff:

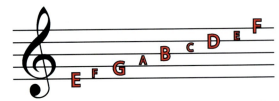

Remember, the music alphabet is: A B C D E F G

Use center F to name the lowest line. **THINK: Before F in the alphabet comes E.**	Play this E key, which is before the F key.	
Use center F to name the second line. **THINK: After F in the alphabet comes G.**	Play this G key, which is after the F key.	
Use the second space A to name the third line. **THINK: After A in the alphabet comes B.**	Play this B key, which is after the A key.	
Use the third space C to name the fourth line. **THINK: After C in the alphabet comes D.**	Play this D key, which is after the C key.	
Use the fourth space E to name the fifth line. **THINK: After E in the alphabet comes F.**	Play this F key, which is after the E key.	

Treble Warm-Ups!

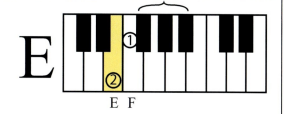

1. Finger 2 locates center F, to the left of the group of 3 black keys.
2. Finger 1 plays the next key to the left: E.

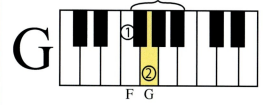

1. Finger 2 locates center F, to the left of the group of 3 black keys.
2. Finger 3 plays the next key to the right: G.

Think of the letter names of the **spaces F A C E** to *name* the lines.

Use the **space keys F A C E** to *locate* the line keys on the keyboard.

"Say each letter name as you play its key!"

1.

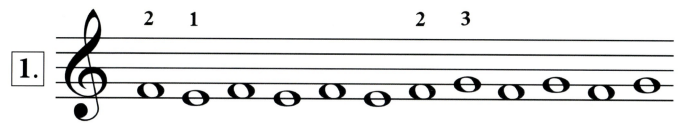

2.

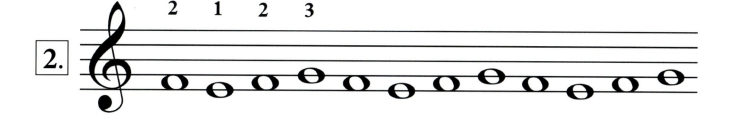

3.

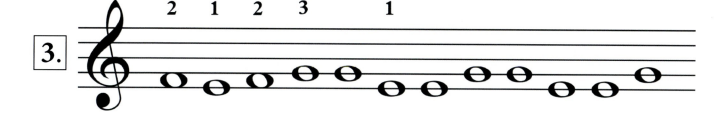

18

4.

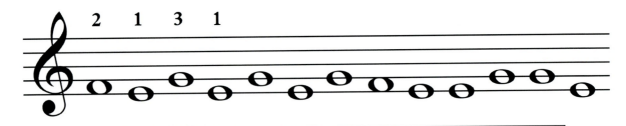

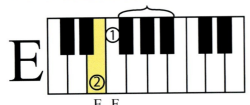

1. Finger 2 locates center F, to the left of the group of 3 black keys.
2. Finger 1 plays the next key to the left: E.

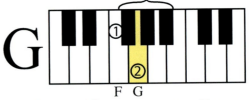

1. Finger 2 locates center F, to the left of the group of 3 black keys.
2. Finger 3 plays the next key to the right: G.

1. Say each letter name as you play its key.
2. Sing the lyrics as you play.

Good Start!

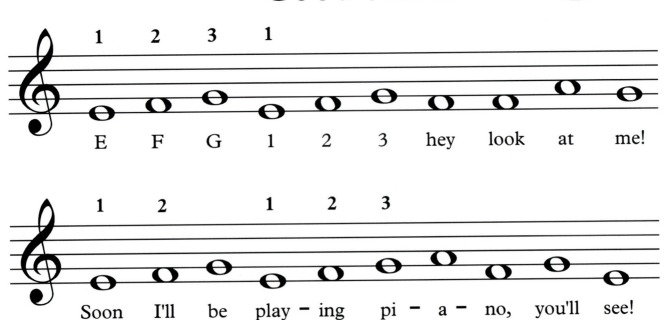

Treble Warm-Ups!

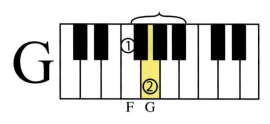

1. Finger 1 locates center F, to the left of the group of 3 black keys.
2. Finger 2 plays the next key to the right: G.

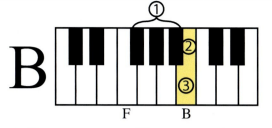

1. Locate center F's group of 3 black keys.
2. Finger 4 bumps the right side of the third black key.
3. Finger 4 slides toward you and plays the B key.

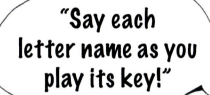

"Say each letter name as you play its key!"

5.
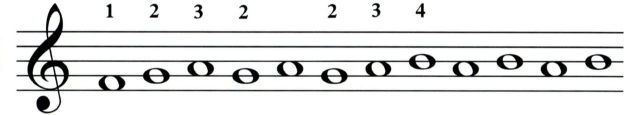

6.
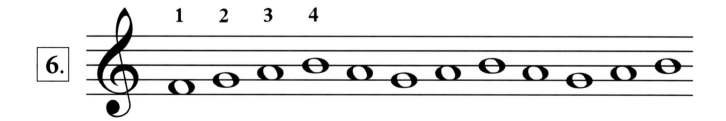

7.
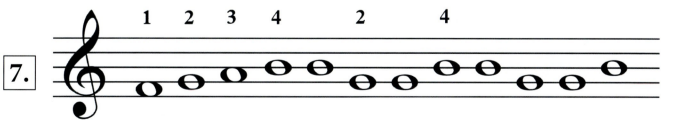

20

8.
   1 2 3 2 3

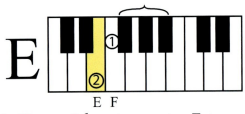
1. Finger 2 locates center F, to the left of the group of 3 black keys.
2. Finger 1 plays the next key to the left: E.

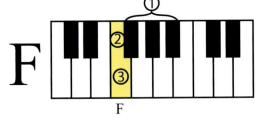
1. Locate center F's group of 3 black keys.
2. Finger 2 bumps the left side of the first black key.
3. Finger 2 slides toward you and plays center F.

1. Say each letter name as you play its key.
2. Sing the lyrics as you play.

High Flying

1 2 3 1 2

I sure would like to have wings so I could fly up high!

1 2 3 1   2   4

High-er and high-er I'd fly un-til I touched the sky!

Treble Warm-Ups!

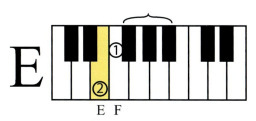

E

1. Finger 2 locates center F, to the left of the group of 3 black keys.
2. Finger 1 plays the next key to the left: E.

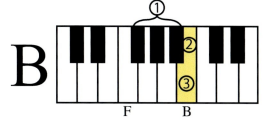

B

1. Locate center F's group of 3 black keys.
2. Finger 5 bumps the right side of the third black key.
3. Finger 5 slides toward you and plays the B key.

"Say each letter name as you play its key!"

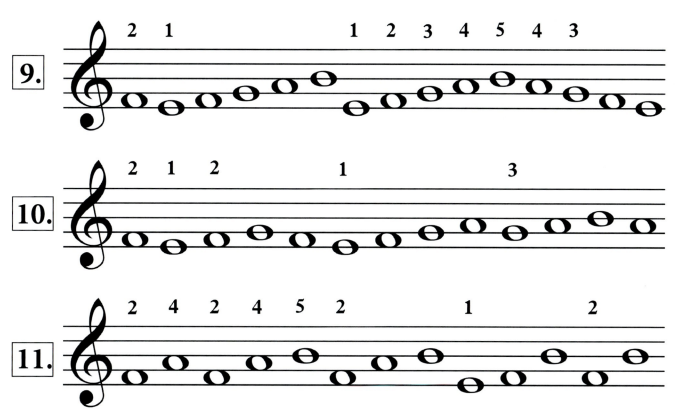

Treble Warm-Ups!

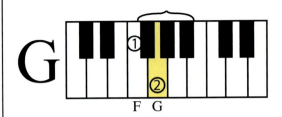

1. Finger 1 locates center F, to the left of the group of 3 black keys.
2. Finger 2 plays the next key to the right: G.

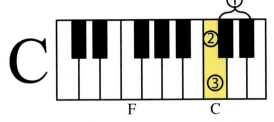

1. Locate the group of 2 black keys to the right of center F.
2. Finger 5 bumps the left side of the first black key.
3. Finger 5 slides toward you and plays the C key.

1. Say each letter name as you play its key.
2. Sing the lyrics as you play.

Hey! Diddle, Diddle

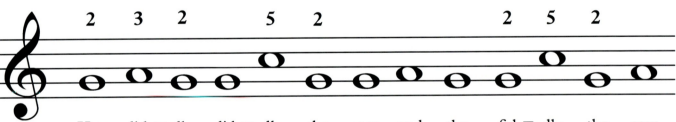

Hey did - dle did - dle, the cat and the fid - dle, the cow

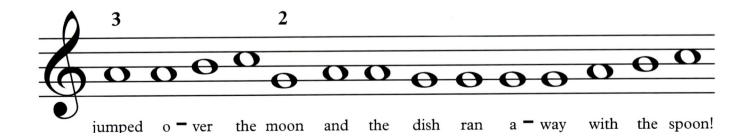

jumped o - ver the moon and the dish ran a - way with the spoon!

Treble Warm-Ups!

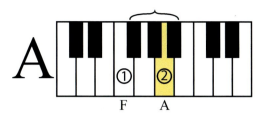

A

1. Finger 1 locates center F, to the left of the group of 3 black keys.
2. Finger 2 hops over to play the A key.

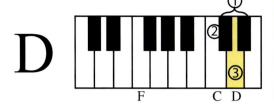

D

1. Locate the group of 2 black keys to the right of center F.
2. Finger 4 bumps the left side of the first black key and slides toward you on the C key.
3. Finger 5 plays the next key to the right: D

"Say each letter name as you play its key!"

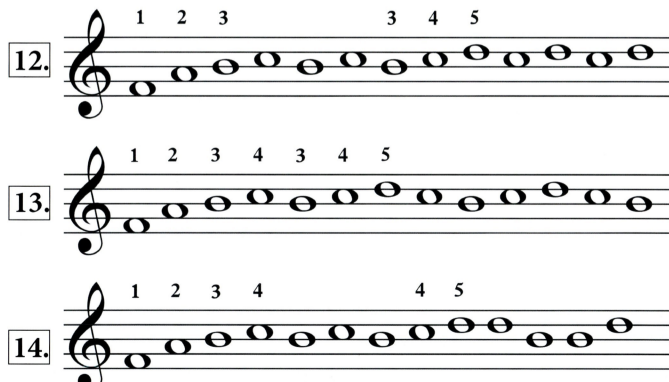

15.

1 2 3 5 3

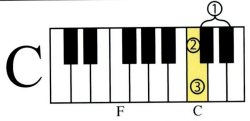

C
1. Locate the group of 2 black keys to the right of center F.
2. Finger 4 bumps the left side of the first black key.
3. Finger 4 slides toward you and plays C.

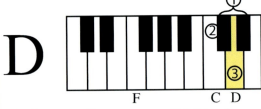

D
1. Locate the group of 2 black keys to the right of center F.
2. Finger 4 bumps the left side of the first black key and slides toward you on the C key.
3. Finger 5 plays the next key to the right: D

1. Say each letter name as you play its key.
2. Sing the lyrics as you play.

Soda Pop

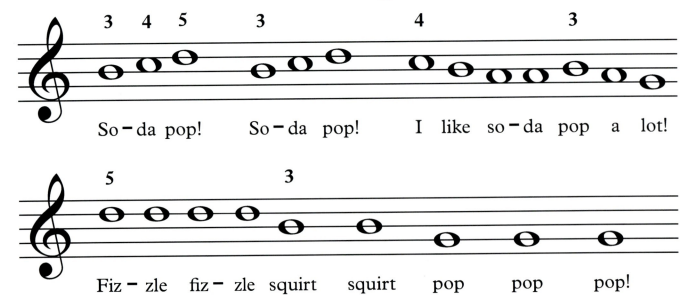

3 4 5   3   4   3

So - da pop! So - da pop! I like so - da pop a lot!

5   3

Fiz - zle fiz - zle squirt squirt pop pop pop!

Before playing Exercise 16, try this fingering when playing up and down the keyboard.
Start on "center F" with your right hand thumb (called "Finger 1").
Use fingers 123, 123, 123 going up the keyboard.
Use fingers 321, 321, 321 going down the keyboard:

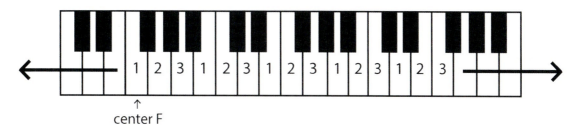

down the keyboard   up the keyboard

Say each letter name as you play its key:

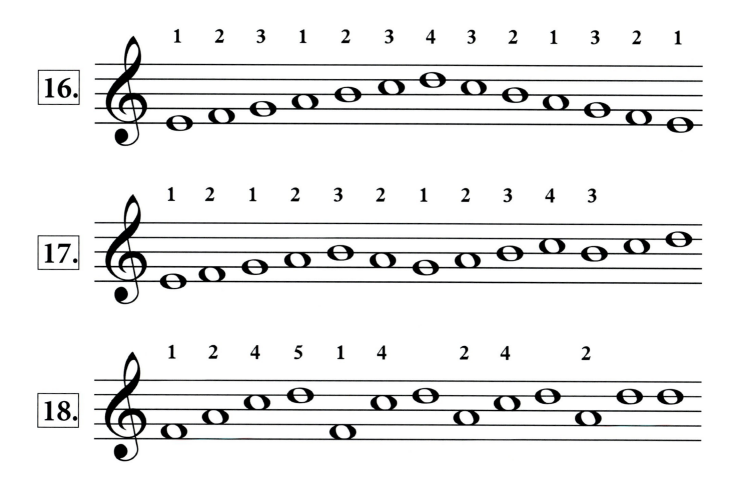

Treble Warm-Ups!

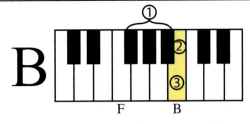

B

1. Locate center F's group of 3 black keys.
2. Finger 3 bumps the right side of the third black key.
3. Finger 3 slides toward you and plays the B key.

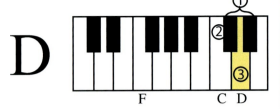

D

1. Locate the group of 2 black keys to the right of center F.
2. Finger 4 bumps the left side of the first black key and slides toward you on the C key.
3. Finger 5 plays the next key to the right: D

1. Say each letter name as you play its key.
2. Sing the lyrics as you play.

Music Math!

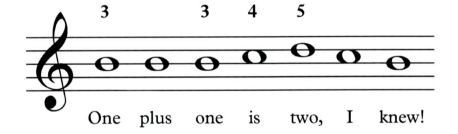

One plus one is two, I knew!

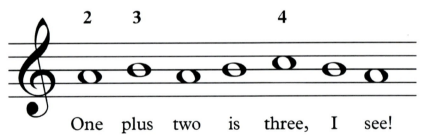

One plus two is three, I see!

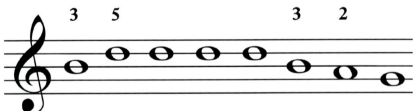

Two plus two is four, and there's more!

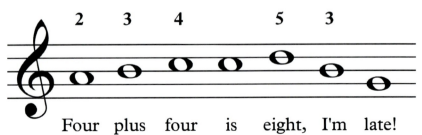

Four plus four is eight, I'm late!

Treble Warm-Ups!

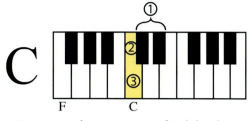

1. Locate the group of 2 black keys to the right of center F.
2. Finger 1 bumps the left side of the first black key.
3. Finger 1 slides toward you and plays the C key.

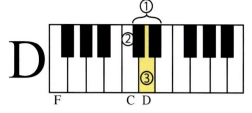

1. Locate the group of 2 black keys to the right of center F.
2. Finger 1 bumps the left side of the first black key and slides toward you on the C key.
3. Finger 2 plays the next key to the right: D

"Say each letter name as you play its key!"

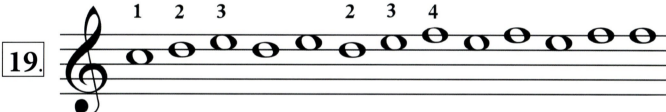

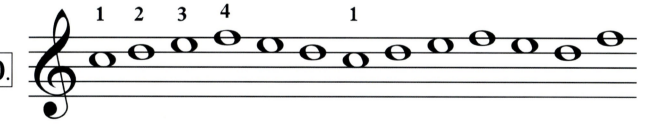

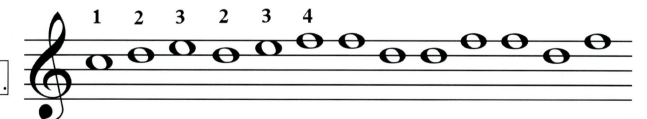

28

22.

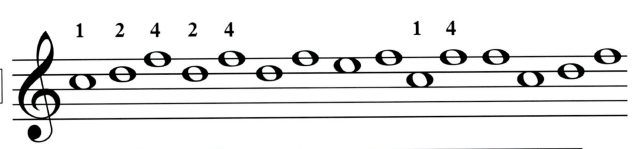

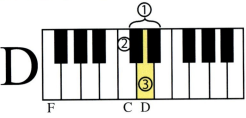

D

1. Locate the group of 2 black keys to the right of center F.
2. Finger 1 bumps the left side of the first black key and slides toward you on the C key.
3. Finger 2 plays the next key to the right: D.

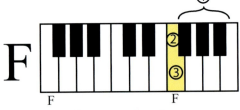

F

1. Locate the next higher group of the 3 black keys to the right of center F.
2. Finger 4 bumps the left side of the first black key.
3. Finger 4 slides toward you and plays the F key.

1. Say each letter name as you play its key.
2. Sing the lyrics as you play.

Campfire Dance

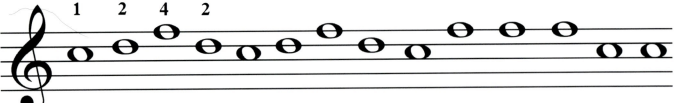

The In-di-ans would dance a-round the bright camp-fires at night!

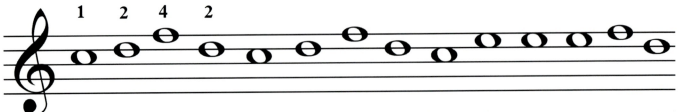

This was a long, long time a-go, but it was sure a sight!

Treble Warm-Ups!

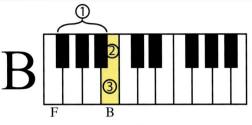

B
1. Locate center F's group of 3 black keys.
2. Finger 1 bumps the right side of the third black key.
3. Finger 1 slides toward you and plays the B key.

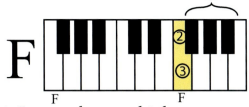

F
1. Locate the next higher group of 3 black keys to the right of center F.
2. Finger 5 bumps the left side of the first black key.
3. Finger 5 slides toward you and plays the F key.

"Say each letter name as you play its key!"

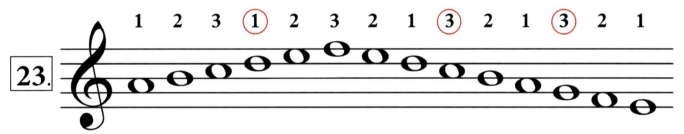

23.

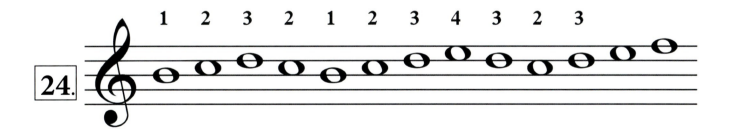

24.

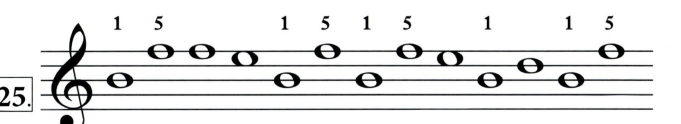

25.

Treble Warm-Ups!

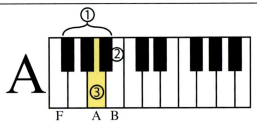

1. Locate center F's group of 3 black keys.
2. Finger 2 bumps the right side of the third black key and slides toward you on the B key.
3. Finger 1 plays the next key to the left: A.

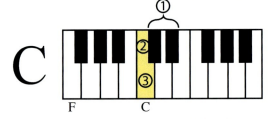

1. Locate the group of 2 black keys to the right of center F.
2. Finger 3 bumps the left side of the first black key.
3. Finger 3 slides toward you and plays the C key.

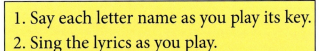

1. Say each letter name as you play its key.
2. Sing the lyrics as you play.

Muddy Socks

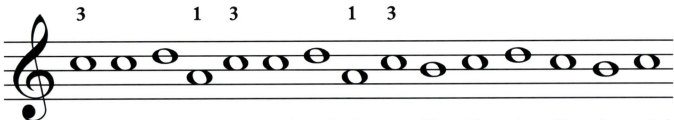

When I find a big mud pud-dle, I like skip-ping lit-tle rocks!

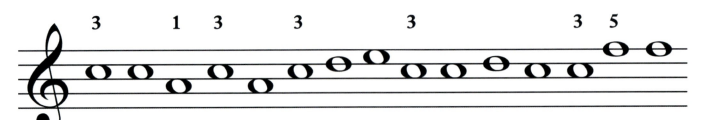

But my Mom gets kind of cra-zy when she sees my mud-dy socks!!

Treble Warm-Ups! 31

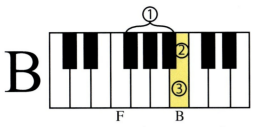

1. Locate center F's group of 3 black keys.
2. Finger 1 bumps the right side of the third black key.
3. Finger 1 slides toward you and plays the B key.

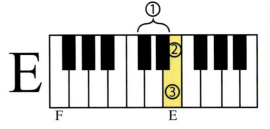

1. Locate the group of 2 black keys to the right of center F.
2. Finger 4 bumps the right side of the second black key.
3. Finger 4 slides toward ou and plays the E key.

"Say each letter name as you play its key!"

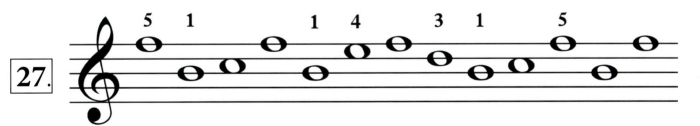

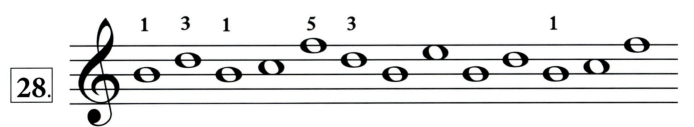

Treble Warm-Ups!

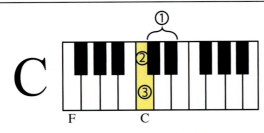

1. Locate the group of 2 black keys to the right of center F.
2. Finger 2 bumps the left side of the first black key.
3. Finger 2 slides toward you and plays the C key.

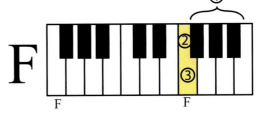

1. Locate the next higher group of the 3 black keys to the right of center F.
2. Finger 5 bumps the left side of the first black key.
3. Finger 5 slides toward you and plays the F key.

1. Say each letter name as you play its key.
2. Sing the lyrics as you play.

A Dinosaur!

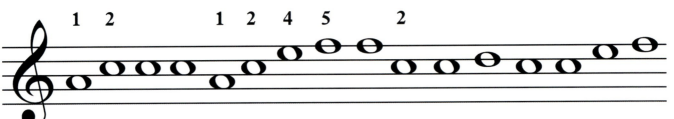

A di-no-saur! I heard him roar! He sounds just like my Dad-dy's snore!

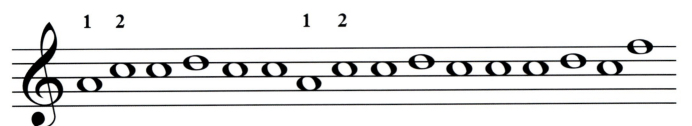

Should I at-tack him with a broom? A di-no-saur in Dad-dy's room!

Treble Warm-Ups! 33

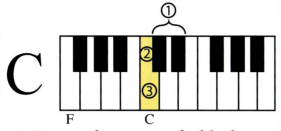

C
1. Locate the group of 2 black keys to the right of center F.
2. Finger 2 bumps the left side of the first black key.
3. Finger 2 slides toward you and plays the C key.

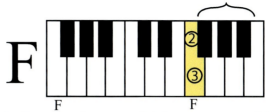

F
1. Locate the next higher group of 3 black keys to the right of center F.
2. Finger 5 bumps the left side of the first black key.
3. Finger 5 slides toward you and plays the F key.

1. Say each letter name as you play its key.
2. Sing the lyrics as you play.

Squishy Sneakers

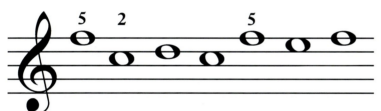

Squish-y sneak-ers don't look nice!

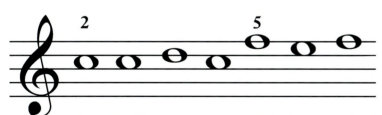

You don't want to sniff them twice!

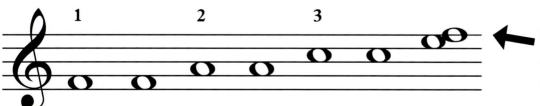

Squish squish tweak tweak squeak squeak ick!!

Play the last 2 keys at the same time!

Treble Warm-Ups!

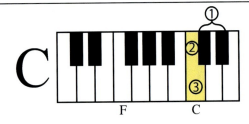

C
1. Locate the group of 2 black keys to the right of center F.
2. Finger 4 bumps the left side of the first black key.
3. Finger 4 slides toward you and plays the C key.

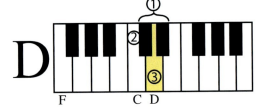

D
1. Locate the group of 2 black keys to the right of center F.
2. Finger 4 bumps the left side of the first black key and slides toward you on the C key.
3. Finger 5 plays the next key to the right: D.

1. Say each letter name as you play its key.
2. Sing the lyrics as you play.

Twinkle, Twinkle, Little Star

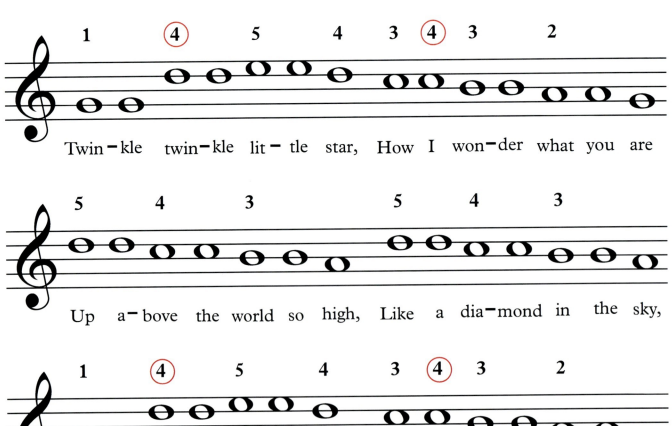

The Bass Clef

35

You have already learned the keys represented by the treble clef's staff, which are played by the right hand. Now look at the keys represented by the lines and spaces of the left hand's staff!

The BASS CLEF SIGN 𝄢 drawn on the staff means to use the left hand to play the keys. This left hand staff is called the BASS CLEF.

It has 5 lines and 4 spaces.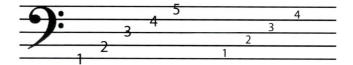

These bass clef lines and spaces represent 9 specific white keys on the keyboard for the left hand to play. These have different letter names than the right hand treble clef lines and spaces.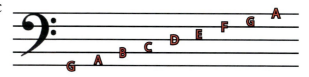

To locate this lowest line G key, begin by finding the right hand's center F key. Play center F with right hand finger 2.

While your right hand is still holding down the center F key, have your left hand find the next closest F key down the keyboard to the left. Remember, F is the white key to the left of the group of 3 black keys. This F key is represented by the fourth line of the bass clef. We will call it "**bass F**".

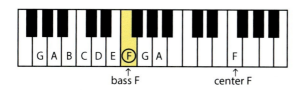 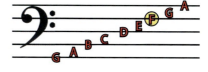

Now with your left hand, play the next lowest F key down the keyboard to the left. You are playing 2 F keys under the right hand's center F key. We will call this key "low F".

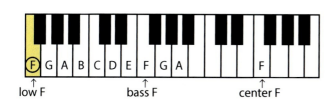 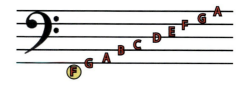

36

Use the left hand's "low F" key to locate the 9 keys represented by the bass clef's lines and spaces. The next key to the right of low F is G, the lowest line of the bass clef.

Play this G key:

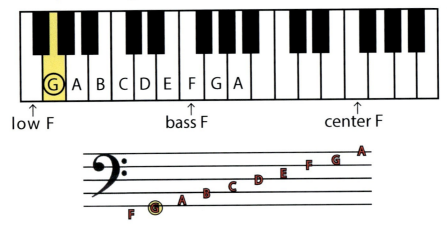

Beginning with the lowest line G key, play and say the letter names of the 9 keys of the bass clef: **G A B C D E F G A**.

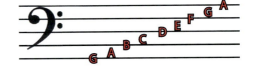

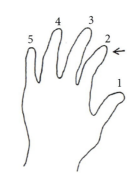

Use Finger 2 of the left hand to play.

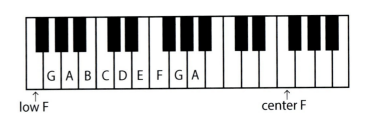

Play these 9 keys using left hand fingers 321 321 321. Say each letter name as you play its key. Notice as you play UP the keyboard (left to right), you are reading UP the staff.	Play these 9 keys backwards using left hand fingers 123 123 123. Say each letter name as you play its key. Notice as you play DOWN the keyboard (right to left), you are reading DOWN the staff.
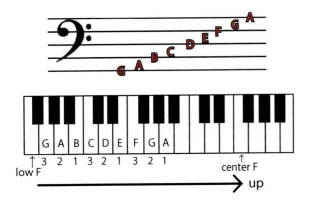	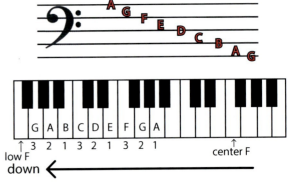

The 4 Bass Clef Spaces   37

To help you locate these keys easily when playing in random order, let the 4 spaces of the staff be your guide.

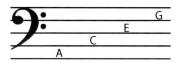

These 4 spaces **A C E G** may be easily remembered by thinking:

All Cows Eat Grass

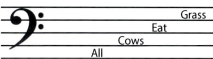

Remember, each line and space of the staff represents a key on the piano keyboard. When you play the keys represented by the 4 spaces of the staff, you will be skipping over the keys represented by the lines of the staff.

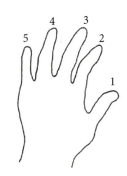

space keys

Play the 4 keys represented by the 4 spaces of the staff **ACEG**, using left hand fingers 5 3 2 1.

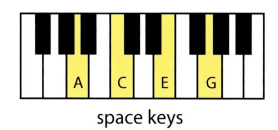

- First play UP the keyboard, left to right, and say each letter name as you play its key.

- Then play DOWN the keyboard, right to left, and say each letter name as you play its key.

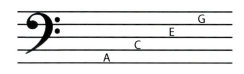
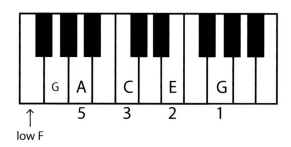

If you have trouble locating the lowest space key A, use "low F" to find the lowest line key G. The next key to the right after the line key G is the space key A.

38

Play By Touch, Not By Looking

To help you play more easily and correctly, try these ways to locate the space keys. Try not to look at the keys as much as possible!

A
1. Locate the 3 black key group to the right of low F.
2. Finger 5 bumps the left side of the first black key and slides toward you on low F.
3. Finger 5 hops over and plays A.

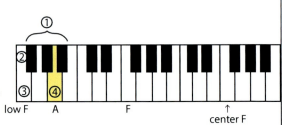

C
1. Locate the group of 2 black keys to the right of low F.
2. Finger 3 bumps the left side of the first black key.
3. Finger 3 slides toward you and plays C.

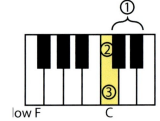

E
1. Locate the group of 2 black keys to the right of low F.
2. Finger 2 bumps the right side of the second black key.
3. Finger 2 slides toward you and plays E.

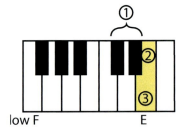

G
1. Finger 2 is on the E key.
2. Finger 1 hops over the next key and plays G.

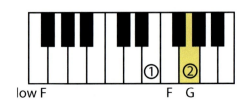

Play the following exercises.

Circles will show you which space key to play:

40

Play the following exercises.

Circles will show you which space key to play:

The Bass Clef Lines   41

Now that you have learned the space keys A C E G, use them to learn the line keys.

Each line of the bass clef is given the letter name of the key it represents on the keyboard. Look at the letter names of the 5 lines of the staff:

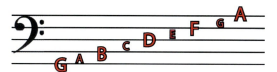

Use the lowest space A to name the lowest line. **THINK: Before the first letter A in the music alphabet comes the last letter G.**		
Use the lowest space A to name the second line. **THINK: After A in the alphabet comes B.**		
Use the second space C to name the third line. **THINK: After C in the alphabet comes D.**		
Use the third space E to name the fourth line. **THINK: After E in the alphabet comes F.**		
Use the fourth space G to name the fifth line. **THINK: After the last letter G in the music alphabet comes the first letter A.**		

Bass Warm-Ups!

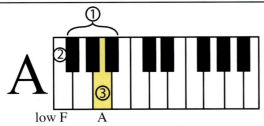

A
low F   A

1. Locate the group of 3 black keys to the right of low F.
2. Finger 5 bumps the left side of the first black key and slides toward you on the F key
3. Finger 3 hops over to play the A key.

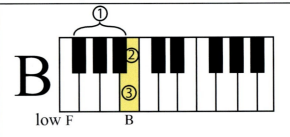

B
low F   B

1. Locate the group of 3 black keys to the right of low F.
2. Finger 2 bumps the right side of the third black key.
3. Finger 2 slides toward you and plays the B key.

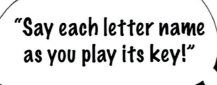

"Say each letter name as you play its key!"

1.
        3   4

2.
        3   4   3   2

3.
        3   4   3   2   4

4.

1. Say each letter name as you play its key.
2. Sing the lyrics as you play.

Bubble Travel

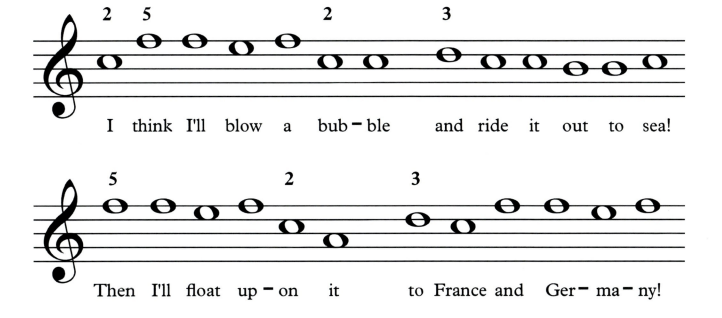

I think I'll blow a bub-ble   and ride it out to sea!

Then I'll float up-on it   to France and Ger-ma-ny!

Bass Warm-Ups!

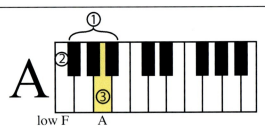

A

1. Locate the group of 3 black keys to the right of low F.
2. Finger 5 bumps the left side of the first black key and slides toward you on the F key.
3. Finger 4 hops over to play the A key.

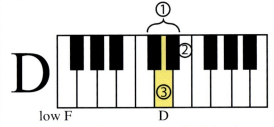

D

1. Locate the group of 2 black keys to the right of low F.
2. Finger 2 bumps the left side of the first black key and slides toward you on the C key.
3. Finger 1 plays the next key to the right: D

"Say each letter name as you play its key!"

45

8.

1. Say each letter name as you play its key.
2. Sing the lyrics as you play.

Don't Be Silly

Don't be sil - ly, you know bet - ter! Cats don't sing and shoes don't ring!

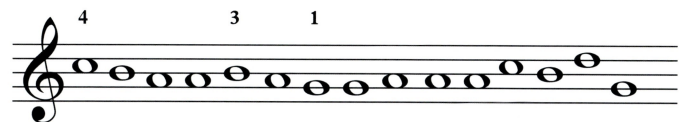

My pet frog won't be a king, and cows don't fly! Do you know why?!

Bass Warm-Ups!

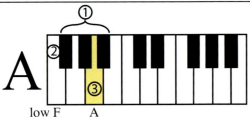

1. Locate the group of 3 black keys to the right of low F.
2. Finger 5 bumps the left side of the first black key and slides toward you on the F key.
3. Finger 4 hops over to play the A key.

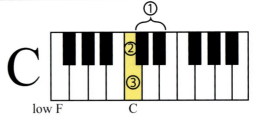

1. Locate the group of 2 black keys to the right of low F.
2. Finger 2 bumps the left side of the first black key.
3. Finger 2 slides toward you and plays the C key.

"Say each letter name as you play its key!"

9.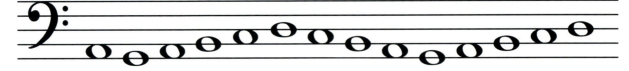

10.

11.

Treble Warm-Ups!

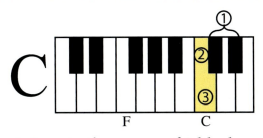

1. Locate the group of 2 black keys to the right of center F.
2. Finger 2 bumps the left side of the first black key.
3. Finger 2 slides toward you and plays the C key.

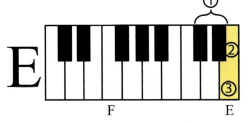

1. Locate the group of 2 black keys to the right of center F.
2. Finger 4 bumps the right side of the second black key.
3. Finger 4 slides toward you and plays the E key.

1. Say each letter name as you play its key.
2. Sing the lyrics as you play.

Yankee Doodle

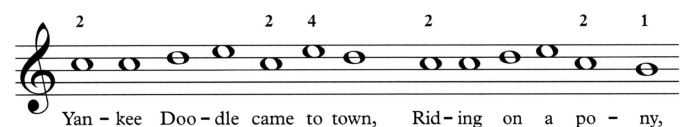

Yan - kee Doo - dle came to town, Rid - ing on a po - ny,

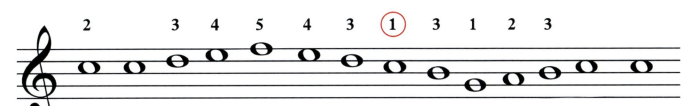

Stuck a fea - ther in his cap and called it ma - ca - ro - ni!

Bass Warm-Ups!

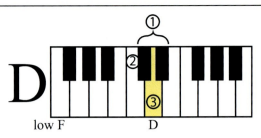

1. Locate the group of 2 black keys to the right of low F.
2. Finger 5 bumps the left side of the first black key and slides toward you on the C key.
3. Finger 4 plays the next key to the right: D

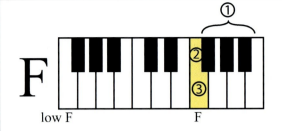

1. Locate the next higher group of 3 black keys to the right of low F.
2. Finger 2 bumps the left side of the first black key.
3. Finger 2 slides toward you and plays the F key.

12.

13.

14.

15.

1. Say each letter name as you play its key.
2. Sing the lyrics as you play.

Fishing with Grandpa

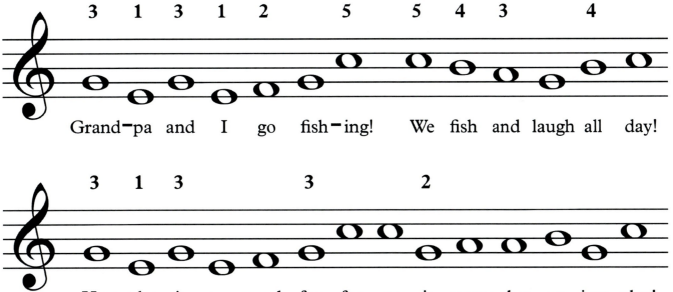

Grand-pa and I go fish-ing! We fish and laugh all day!
He makes it so much fun for me it seems that we just play!

Bass Warm-Ups!

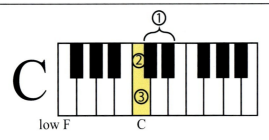

1. Locate the group of 2 black keys to the right of low F.
2. Finger 4 bumps the left side of the first black key.
3. Finger 4 slides toward you and plays the C key.

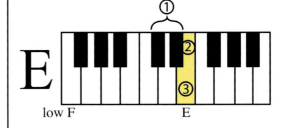

1. Locate the next higher group of 2 black keys to the right of low F.
2. Finger 2 bumps the right side of the second black key.
3. Finger 2 slides toward you and plays the E key.

"Say each letter name as you play its key!"

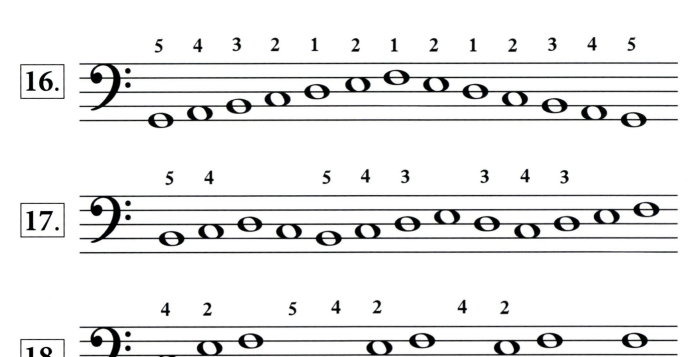

Treble Warm-Ups! 51

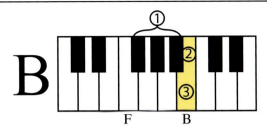

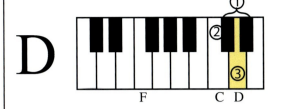

1. Locate the group of 3 black keys to the right of center F.
2. Finger 2 bumps the right side of the third black key.
3. Finger 2 slides toward you and plays the B key.

1. Locate the group of 2 black keys to the right of center F.
2. Finger 3 bumps the left side of the first black key and slides toward you on the C key.
3. Finger 4 plays the next key to the right: D.

1. Say each letter name as you play its key.
2. Sing the lyrics as you play.

This Old Man

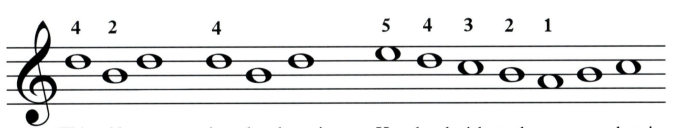

This old man, he played one! He played nick nack on my drum!

Nick nack pad—dy whack! Give the dog a bone! This old man came roll—ing home!

Bass Warm-Ups!

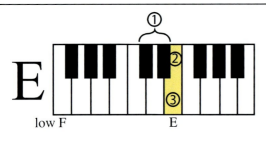

1. Locate the group of 2 black keys to the right of low F.
2. Finger 4 bumps the right side of the second black key.
3. Finger 4 slides toward you and plays the E key.

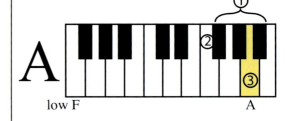

1. Locate the next higher group of 3 black keys to the right of low F.
2. Finger 3 bumps the left side of the first black key and slides toward you on the F key.
3. Finger 1 hops over to play the A key.

"Say each letter name as you play its key!"

19.

20.

21.

22.

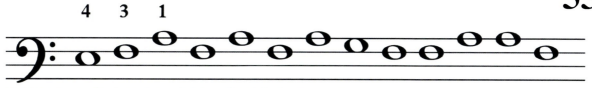

1. Say each letter name as you play its key.
2. Sing the lyrics as you play.

Seaside

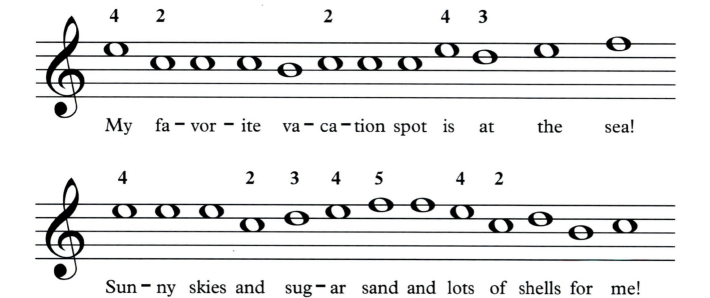

My fa-vor-ite va-ca-tion spot is at the sea!

Sun-ny skies and sug-ar sand and lots of shells for me!

Bass Warm-Ups!

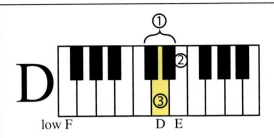

D

1. Locate the group of 2 black keys to the right of low F.
2. Finger 4 bumps the right side of the second black key and slides toward you on the E key.
3. Finger 5 plays the next key to the left: D.

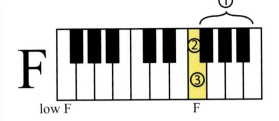

F

1. Locate the next higher group of 3 black keys to the right of low F.
2. Finger 3 bumps the left side of the first black key.
3. Finger 3 slides toward you and plays the F key.

"Say each letter name as you play its key!"

Treble Warm-Ups! 55

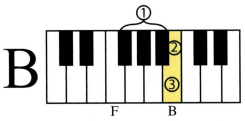

1. Locate the group of 3 black keys to the right of center F.
2. Finger 3 bumps the right side of the third black key.
3. Finger 3 slides toward you and plays the B key.

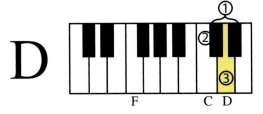

1. Locate the group of 2 black keys to the right of center F.
2. Finger 4 bumps the left side of the first black key and slides toward you on the C key.
3. Finger 5 plays the next key to the right: D.

1. Say each letter name as you play its key.
2. Sing the lyrics as you play.

Pop! Goes the Weasel!

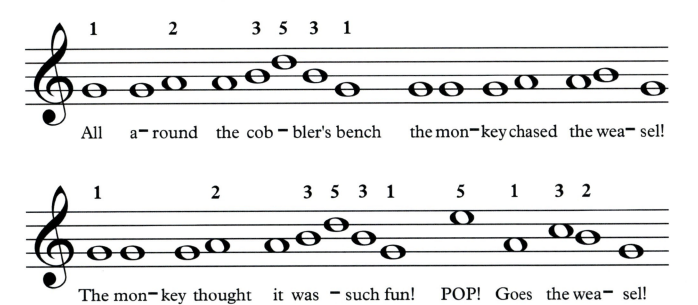

Bass Warm-Ups!

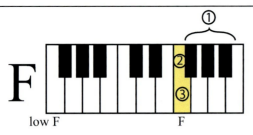

1. Locate the next higher group of 3 black keys to the right of low F.
2. Finger 3 bumps the left side of the first black key.
3. Finger 3 slides toward you and plays the F key.

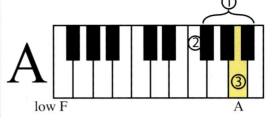

1. Locate the next higher group of 3 black keys to the right of low F.
2. Finger 3 bumps the left side of the first black key and slides toward you on the F key.
3. Finger 1 hops over to play the A key.

"Say each letter name as you play its key!"

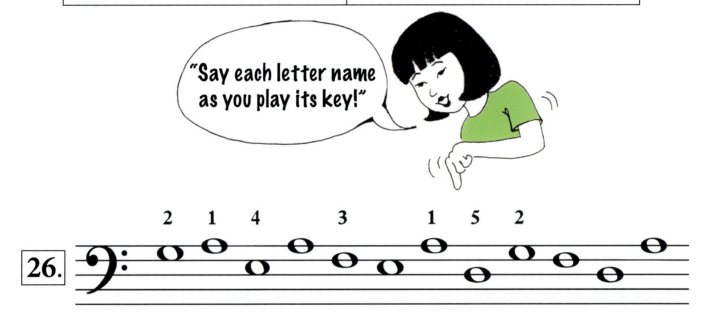

Melody and Accompaniment

57

The tune of a song, to which you sing the words, is called the **MELODY**. Most often the right hand plays the melody, written on the treble clef.

While the right hand plays the melody, the left hand plays the **ACCOMPANIMENT**. These are keys that sound well played with the melody.

The Grand Staff

To make it easier to play the melody and accompaniment together, the treble clef and the bass clef are joined with a BRACKET and are called a GRAND STAFF. At the end of the song is a DOUBLE BAR LINE.

Each bass circle is played *at the same time* as the treble circle directly above it and *is held down until* the next bass circle is played.

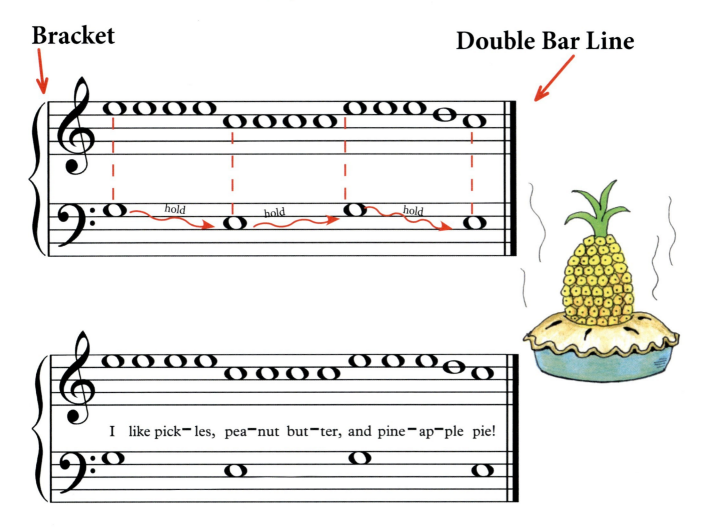

1. Say each letter name as you play its key.
2. Sing the lyrics as you play.

Soda Pop

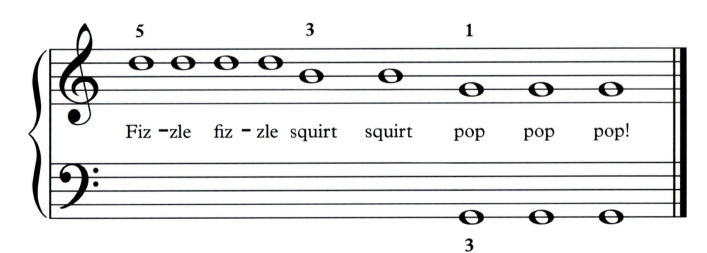

1. Say each letter name as you play its key.
2. Sing the lyrics as you play.

Mary Had a Little Lamb

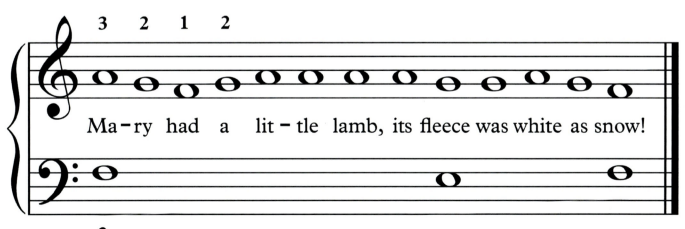

1. Say each letter name as you play its key.
2. Sing the lyrics as you play.

London Bridge

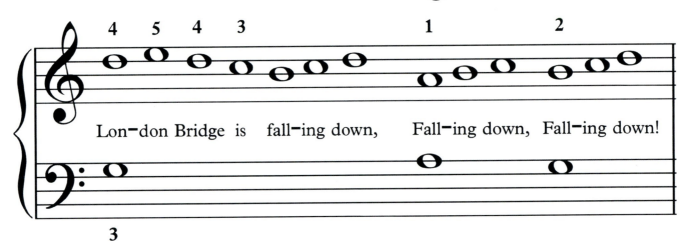

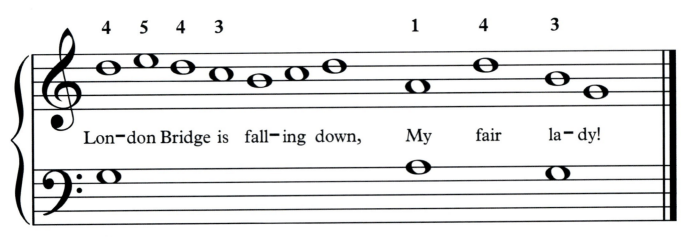

61

1. Say each letter name as you play its key.
2. Sing the lyrics as you play.

Yankee Doodle

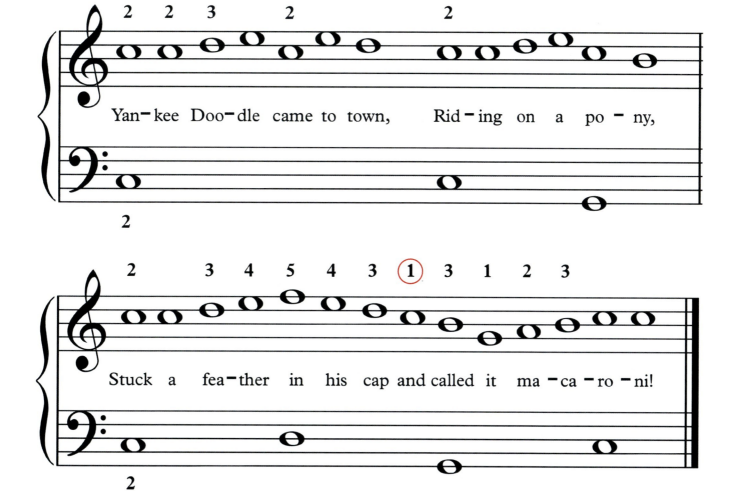

1. Say each letter name as you play its key.
2. Sing the lyrics as you play.

Hey! Diddle, Diddle

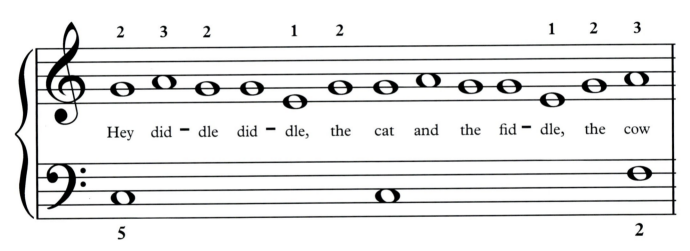

Hey did-dle did-dle, the cat and the fid-dle, the cow

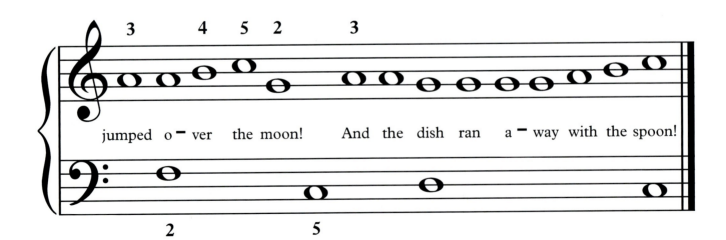

jumped o-ver the moon! And the dish ran a-way with the spoon!

1. Say each letter name as you play its key.
2. Sing the lyrics as you play.

This Old Man

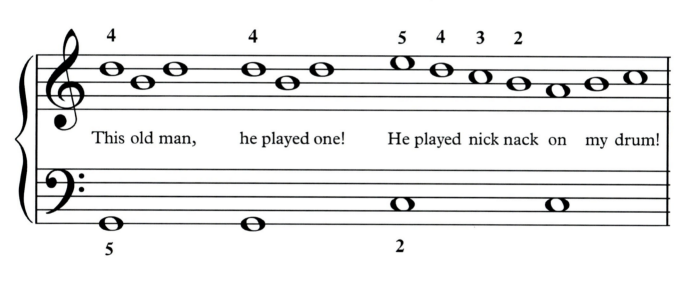

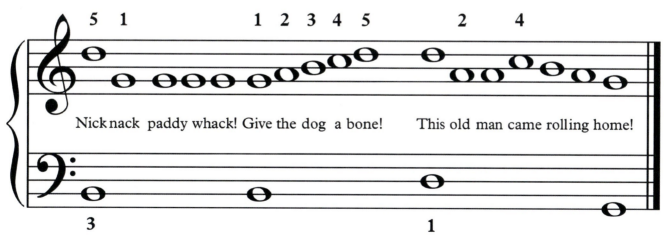

Twinkle, Twinkle, Little Star

Congratulations, you have finished the book!

The next book can be ordered from Amazon.com

Made in the USA
Columbia, SC
29 April 2021